MW01674566

Lifeology:

Tips for Living a Better, Healthier Life

by

Zachary Curtis

DORRANCE
PUBLISHING CO
EST. 1920
PITTSBURGH, PENNSYLVANIA 15238

The contents of this work, including, but not limited to, the accuracy of events, people, and places depicted; opinions expressed; permission to use previously published materials included; and any advice given or actions advocated are solely the responsibility of the author, who assumes all liability for said work and indemnifies the publisher against any claims stemming from publication of the work.

All Rights Reserved
Copyright © 2022 by Zachary Curtis

No part of this book may be reproduced or transmitted, downloaded, distributed, reverse engineered, or stored in or introduced into any information storage and retrieval system, in any form or by any means, including photocopying and recording, whether electronic or mechanical, now known or hereinafter invented without permission in writing from the publisher.

Dorrance Publishing Co
585 Alpha Drive
Suite 103
Pittsburgh, PA 15238
Visit our website at *www.dorrancebookstore.com*

ISBN: 978-1-6393-7150-1
eISBN: 978-1-6393-7961-3

Lifeology:

Tips for Living a Better, Healthier Life

TABLE OF CONTENTS

INTRODUCTION

Welcome to Lifeology: Tips for Living a Better, Healthier Life. I would first like to salute you for having the interest to improve and enhance your life. Self-improvement is not an easy thing, and too many people are comfortable with staying the same. Along the journey in life, especially in this modern society, there are a lot of distractions in the world.

We are constantly battling with these distractions every day in our lives. Since I was young, I have always experienced a lot of situations that provide me with the motivation, knowledge, and insight on this life experience. I always knew that there is more to life than just the average things that are sold to us by various sources.

Having an interest to help others and spread the truth gave me the motivation to write this book, along with my spirit guiding me too as well. Lifeology is the study of life. We all have unique experiences, yet we are very connected. Our differences should not divide us, whether physical or not. I will share some of my experiences along with the keys in the chapters of this book.

While reading this book, have an open mind and acknowledge that there is always a learning experience in life. A wise man once told me "You don't know what you don't know." This book will not only provide tips and valuable gems but will also uplift you to inspire your ascension.

Let's get on this journey
to live a better, healthier life.

CHAPTER 1: KNOW THYSELF

Every being on this earth is born with a specific blueprint or plan that comes equipped. Within your DNA lies greatness that has its existence through many generations of your family and bloodline. Your DNA will be very similar yet different from those to whom you are related. What your parents possess, you will acquire that and much more. With all the distractions around us, we can quickly lose track of that blueprint and many qualities already within us. This current status is where knowing yourself comes in to play.

Knowing thyself means being conscious and aware of the true self and not getting caught in the "ego trap. It is also living in alignment with what one is sent to earth in this lifetime to accomplish. "Every one of us has a purpose or calling that we must attend. When we do not attend to this purpose or calling, we may feel a sense of resistance inside that lets us know something is missing, something more significant. When we know ourselves, we are closer to our natural state. We also know others and gain a better understanding of human nature.

Natural State

The natural state is the original, synchronized form that is within us. This state goes along with the specific and unique blueprint that identifies you. When we look at nature, we know that everything apart of it knows its functions. For example, water has many uses, but it still gives life and a sense of living with every service. In our natural states as humans, we become the best version of ourselves, the God or Goddess within. We are made in God's image.

The God or Goddess that is within will reveal itself when the time is right. The process isn't all peaches and cream. When the divine part is revealed, there's usually a spiritual awakening that takes place along with lots of healing. This period of healing and transformation is to make you better and be harmonious in the long term. When an issue at hand doesn't have the proper care and attention, it may continue manifesting until resolved. Great position and divinity require great responsibility.

The majority of individuals are in a dormant state and are not aware of it. When in a dormant state, we are not able to access our higher self. There are various factors, such as diet, mental awareness, emotions, and necessary actions. The previous factors are just a few examples and are continually being manipulated to keep us in a "dormant" state. In turn, the manipulation and confusion of our inner divine block us from reaching the natural state.

When we are in our natural state, life becomes more manageable, and a state of flow and fulfillment is reached. In this natural state, manifesting becomes easier due to having less confusion and being able to have positive thinking. I have learned that manifesting is a key to having what you want in life.

Manifesting is simply something that is clear to the eye or mind and will make your life better. Whether we realize it or not, we manifest every day, and being in our natural state will easily bring us more peace and positivity. Your expectations in life are what you will end up manifesting. What you expect out of life or anything is what you will usually get.

When we are in our natural state, we permit others to get in their natural state. Even though not every individual will be aware of their natural state, you can serve as an inspiration to those who are interested. In this state, we are one, but not necessarily equal with everything that is around us. The natural state is similar to a body where all aspects work in harmony together.

We shouldn't go against nature or our natural state. We should instead connect with nature and learn to embrace nature and our natural, authentic selves.

Finding Yourself

Throughout your journey, I know there have been a few times when you feel that you've lost yourself and don't recognize the person you see in the mirror. You may have a lot of questions and inquiries in mind at this point. This time is a normal process and gives us the strength that we will need. When you feel that you've lost yourself, this is a signal of growth and that it is time to take some action. The action is a reference to finding yourself.

Finding yourself takes time, effort, trial, and patience. It doesn't come overnight or in a quick second. One must take on, trust, and embrace the process of finding themselves. This process can be on-going and have different periods; it all depends on the individual. It would be best if one puts in the effort to find themselves and know who they are if they have limited knowledge of their true selves. Even the subtle and superficial levels of action will help. Some good ways to start finding yourself are meditation, journaling, and conscious breathing. These ways are overall efficient and will bring results when combined with desire and consistency. One must find the best ways that work for them.

Everything is done with intention. God makes every individual different for a specific reason. No human being knows this reason. Therefore, it is essential to find yourself. Finding yourself leads to you more to your natural and higher self, creating a better life for you and those around you. Having things in order makes for a better condition.

When you find yourself and know yourself, the world around you and your perspective will shift. One will begin to look at the world with an open mind and not limit themselves. Having a closed mind creates stagnation and hinders progress in one's life. When you open your mind, you start to find your natural self. When you find yourself, you open your world, leading to attracting the things you desire. Achieving your desires opens your reality. More people, opportunities, and other great things will gravitate towards you.

There is a small percentage of the population today that truly knows themselves. The world constantly bombards us with distractions that work against us in the long run. Examples of these "distractions" include social media, television, and the news. These examples all have one thing in common, which is propaganda. Propaganda is used to change the minds of the consumer. This is why the government makes these distractions: easy-to-access, cheap, or free of charge. Television tells lies to your vision and promotes many false narratives. The news has a primary purpose of fostering fear and confusion more than shining light on the positive things occurring in the world. If television or the news would push more motivational and positive content, I believe that television would change the lives of those who watch these sources for the better. Social media can be time-consuming and destroying mentally, physically, or emotionally if used for the wrong reasons or without a purpose.

The decisions of the consumer are the primary factor that determines how these "distractions" are managed. Social media, the news, and television are not entirely negative, and they have their positives. It is up to you to determine: the type of content you consume, how frequently you consume the content, and the reason behind consumption. Everything that you do should be done with intent and motive. Make sure to surround yourself with that which what you want to be. It takes finding yourself to know who you want to be and what you truly desire.

"The chosen ones choose themselves." -Anonymous.

Who Am I?

A great question that always arises within every one of us is "Who Am I?" This question comes up while we are living our lives. "I" is the individual within a body. We are spiritual beings living in a physical body. The physical body is a vehicle, and we are the drivers of the vehicle. Variables such as our names, date of birth, and physical characteristics do not fully define us. They are just variables added to the "I."

When we recognize that we are spiritual beings, we unlock the doors to endless possibilities. We begin to take care of ourselves in all aspects of our lives and begin to live. The knowledge of self inspires one to find balance and enhance their "I."

CHAPTER 2: BUILD THYSELF

Once one knows themselves, they must continue and build themselves. A strong foundation is needed to build a house. The foundation sets the stage for the process. In this case, one needs to find and know themselves to have something to build on. The Law of Vibration states: "Nothing rests; everything moves; everything vibrates. Without movement, there is stagnation.

Comfort Zones

To achieve any goals you have in life, you will have to undergo some risk. These risks involve getting uncomfortable. Comfort is similar to a drug. Too much comfort over an extended time may cause addiction and hinder one's progress. Comfort needs its balance, just as everything in life does.

The comfort zone consists of things that one is familiar with and is a safe space. The comfort zone can minimize stress and pressure on an individual when expanded. The main problem with comfort zones is that too many individuals get stuck in this zone. When stuck in the comfort zone, one is limiting themselves to the great possibility that exists within. We all have the power to change our realities. Even if one falls victim to getting stuck inside of their comfort zone, they can change that as well.

The comfort zone affects our spirit and usually is comprised of habits and routines that no longer serve us. When we are in our comfort zone for an extended period, our spirit lets us know something is not right. The spirit is simply the real "I" of an individual. The spirit is divine and full of essence, connecting to one's higher self. When the spirit is not intact, it transfers over to the physical. Many individuals who are always in their comfort zones are more likely to encounter bred forms of fear, anxiety, and depression. If you feel a sensation within your body (gut feeling) that you are not fulfilling something and ignore it, consequences will arise.

The remedy to overcoming being stuck inside the comfort zone is: action and expanding zones. Many successful individuals get outside of their comfort zone consistently. They utilize action and develop their zones. The action starts with one reflecting on their life and knowing more is possible. It is recommended that one starts getting uncomfortable by doing small tasks that they may not normally do. This does not mean to do anything that you know is not good and will do more harm than benefit for an individual or the collective. Examples of small tasks, in a situational form, may include reading a book when you want to watch TV, taking cold showers, adding a new workout to your routine, and fasting.

When one continually does new things, they will eventually become comfortable with the once unknown. This reboot occurs through repetition, muscle memory, and the neurological pathways experiencing a chance to grow. This process will, in turn, expand your comfort zone and other zones. Just because one's comfort zone extends doesn't justify staying in it. One must continue to "KEEP LEARNING AND IMPROVING."

"Letting Go"

When it comes to building thyself, one must let go of any people, places, thoughts, or things holding one back. The longer these non-beneficial factors are kept, the more detrimental they will become. We may not see the results of holding onto things longer than they are needed instantly, but as the saying goes: "You reap what you sow." A great example of this is shown in farming. If a farmer were to plant a tomato seed and expected cucumbers, it would be impossible. The farmer still has to take care of the tomato plant to yield the best results possible. When the process is followed, the farmer will, in turn, have a great harvest.

Whatever we send out into the universe comes back to us. Every action has an equal or opposite reaction. This law leads to the topic of thought. One must first understand that everything starts with the mind. The Hermetic Principle, "The Principle of Mentalism," states: "All is mind; the universe is mental." When your mind is healthy, and you send out healthy, positive thoughts, you reap the positive. Thought waves travel!

How does this relate to letting go? Whatever thought one sends out, good or bad, returns to the person. A common mistake that many make when it comes to manifesting is holding on to a thought. One should "visualize" clearly what they want and use focus and discipline to take action. The more time one spends thinking, the longer it will take to receive, hence wasting time taking action. On the other hand, when negative thoughts are let go, positive thoughts are now welcome to come freely.

Therefore, when we let go of the negative or anything that no longer serves us, we open many doors. Blockages are now removed, and the path continues. "LET GO AND LET IT FLOW." When one lets go of that which is unneeded and removes blockages, they can live in the present and enjoy the moment.

The Application

Application is a necessity when it comes to knowledge and wisdom. It is also what separates a knowledgeable being from a wise being. Knowledge and wisdom are very similar, yet there are levels. One who knows is only conscious of something and has broken the barrier of ignorance. The wise being takes the knowledge further and applies it to their life. They use it in a way that builds themselves and their reality. Wasted knowledge is like wasted time. Be wise with your knowledge and apply what you learn. Experience and knowledge are two significant assets in life.

Repetition and routine are huge factors when it comes to the application. Knowledge should transfer to actions. Once something is done and repeated over-and-over, it becomes a habit. Everyone should desire to have good habits, and this desire will serve as the start to a healthy routine. A healthy routine will help one live the life they want and even build willpower and discipline. Repetition can also boost our memory. One simple trick is to take what you learn and apply it in your everyday life—all effort matters. Repetition has the power to change our neurological pathways in our brains, so one must choose wisely what they do on a consistent basis.

When you first start applying what you've learned, every time may not be successful. This impatience will cause some to stop having the desire to learn and apply. If the desire to learn and apply is not present, one runs the risk of fearing anything new or unusual. This fear will only hold an individual back from achieving their goals. If you find yourself in this situation or feel a leaning towards it, ask yourself:

"What is the cause of this problem?"

"What can I do to solve it?"

The ONLY way to break fear, in general, is by **taking action**. Every situation and life experience has learning opportunities, and one should always use these for growth. Going through these experiences will teach you the right ways to apply, so fear should be limited. You never know until you DO.

Everything that is taught and received has the possibility of not being entirely accurate. The potential for inaccuracy and semi-truths is where the individual must evaluate the knowledge obtained. If you have a gut feeling that something is not right, there's a massive possibility that it's not right. The gut is like another brain in the body and, of course, affects the spirit. That is an example of a way one might evaluate the validity of knowledge. Continue doing research and reflect on the knowledge as well.

When you apply the knowledge and build yourself, you open many doors for yourself and others. You are now able to teach others. Teaching is one of the many forms of giving. When you give to others, you give to yourself as well. Apply the principle of "giving freely without expectation, and you will build yourself and live a better life." When you use the application, you are now walking the walk and will receive desired results.

One should always seek to improve. Never become entirely comfortable. Comfort over time can lead to stagnation, as stated before. Keep your balance and have the mindset that you are only in real competition with yourself. One can be their biggest fan or their worst enemy.

When you have faith and apply, the world around you will begin to comply.

CHAPTER 3: MIND OVER MATTER

Everything in life is connected. The mind, body, and spirit are all reflections of one another.

Everything starts with the mind. When you put your mind to something, you can do it, and it'll be the driving force that sparks your desire and faith. The mental aspect will reflect in the spiritual realm and the physical world. "Mind over Matter" is when one has excellent control over one physical body through a keen use of the mind. Control your mind, and you control your reality.

How Everything Starts with the Mind

The hermetic principle of Mentalism states: "All is mind. The universe is mental." The mind births, the mind creates. Many of the world's great innovators first had an idea, which they then made and expressed in a physical form. God gifted everyone on the Earth with a mind for a reason. The mind is like a powerhouse. It stores information, provides awareness, and generates great ideas. If the mind is a powerhouse, it can have a significant effect on the body. When the mind is used correctly, the right amount of power and energy will be sent to the body. The subconscious mind is the part of this powerhouse that many should pay more attention to; it is a fascinating part of the mind.

Every time you think a thought, you are sending thought waves into the universe. Thoughts eventually return to the sender. Think of how the waves in the ocean send out ripples; they may move to the shore for a moment, then they will settle back and return to the water where the waves began. Thought waves travel and are faster than the speed of light. Thoughts can travel up to 120 miles per second.

The Subconscious Mind

The subconscious mind is the mind that takes in information via the senses- touch, taste, smell, sight, and audio. These senses, along with the experiences we encounter throughout life, create memories. Whether one likes it or not, the subconscious mind is always listening and receiving information. This part of the mind is susceptible and doesn't judge the information, whether good or bad. Even when we are getting our rest, the subconscious mind is still moving and working. On the other hand, the conscious mind is selective, and it is easier to control what enters and exits directly.

The more emotions that are mixed with thoughts, the easier it is to plant things into the subconscious mind.

Since the subconscious mind is continuous and highly active, it is vital to program it correctly. One has two choices when it comes to programming- to program or be programmed. Many companies, tel-lie-vision programs, and commercials know the power behind programming and take advantage of it. They will usually show their image continuously to plant the thought of purchasing in the consumer's mind and get people to buy their products. Some of the products that we think are our favorites, in reality, might not be our favorites. We may have seen the product so often, and usually, external sources put the thought of purchasing in our subconscious mind. One must know the thoughts that originate within them from those elsewhere. This analysis is done by taking control of your mind and keeping a high vibration. When one programs their subconscious, they can live a better life, have better thoughts within their conscious mind, and manifest things quicker, to name a few.

Reprogramming the subconscious mind requires three main components:

Commitment

Repetition

The Correct Programs

Commitment: The first component to reprogram the subconscious mind is commitment. One has to realize that it takes time and effort to reprogram something that has been programmed continuously, mainly by outside sources, whether good or not, right from the time we were born. The programming started while we were in the wombs of our mothers and continues today.

To commit, one has to take the realization into account and use various ways to reprogram.

Examples of Ways to Reprogram Your Subconscious Mind
Affirmations
Sound
Writing

There are many ways to reprogram the subconscious mind. The ways listed above are the primary methods used that are proven to help. I encourage the reader to be creative as well.

Affirmations

With saying affirmations, make sure they are something that you have an interest in becoming or manifesting into your life. The faith in your affirmations along with the action will make them come true. Dreams can come true. When saying affirmations, use the words **"I am, and now."** When you use "I am," this automatically directs it to yourself and puts you at a higher vibration. The "I AM" frequency is very potent and, when used correctly, will uplift the individual. Using **"now"** with this phrase lets your subconscious know that you already have your wish.

When using affirmations, whether written, spoken, drawn, etc., it is important to speak positively. When the subconscious hears bad, it brings bad. For non-positive things, place not in front of it. (EX. I am not healthy.) When you place not in the phrase instead of saying another phrase, it brings the state of being healthy to you while still acknowledging how you're feeling.

Sound is another useful example of a way to reprogram your subconscious mind. When the right vibrations are applied within sound, it has the power to heal. The majority of today's music, even on streaming platforms such as Apple Music, Spotify, and YouTube, does the opposite and is typically tuned at 440 Hz. For example, classical music and jazz are two genres with a higher vibration than mainstream hip-hop.

Over time the listener may not feel the effect of listening to this frequency, yet the elites strategically use it to program. This statement is not saying to stop listening to your favorite song. Instead, it is a sign to be more aware. You could even listen to your favorite song in the background by saying your affirmations.

> Sometimes when we've been accustomed to doing something so long, it is easy to become numb to the real feeling or quickly feel a difference.

Furthermore, writing improves and enhances your memory. The muscle movement and energy behind the action connect with the brain. When learning how to write letters, words, and sentences, one would have to know what hand to write with and put in the effort to learn how to write. The metaphysics (beyond the physical) of writing goes deep. A good example of this is using a no. 2 pencils when writing. The lead in a number 2 pencil has s high vibration since it is a metal and will help manifestations occur quicker. When writing with the goal to program, writing things repeatedly and intention helps the message stick to your brain.

Repetition

When an action is done over and over in a constructive pattern, this is known as repetition. Repetition brings about a connection between the person and the thing(s) that one is doing. Think of working out, for example. When one is in the gym for their reason, the person does a certain number of reps for each exercise. Reps are repetition, and the muscle is being trained to use the effort to achieve the goal.

Repetition does require work and effort to be successful. Time will vary depending on the person, yet anything done repetitively will yield some result. When it comes to reprogramming the subconscious mind and implanting new information, it is crucial to be committed to using repetition. At first, the task may seem difficult. Over time, the task will become more comfortable and will have the appearance of being done with little to no effort, and this is programming within itself. The best people in their crafts, fields, industries, etc., seem to do things effortlessly and almost perfect. This "perfection" arises from putting in the proper effort over time, continuously sharpening their blade, and making great use of their time.

A few examples were listed under the commitment of reprogramming the subconscious mind, primarily through affirmations. When the best methods are found for you, you must use those in repetition. It is said to take 21 days to form a habit. This statement is true yet can vary based on the person when it comes to reprogramming the subconscious. Quality over quantity should be the mindset. The more something is done in repetition, the better the results. Even the "busiest" individuals can take the time out of their day to engage in some activity using repetition.

Things that improve us are worth the time, energy, and effort. These positive investments will bring the best results. We should sacrifice short-term gratification for long-term success.

As long as one takes action is what matters.

The Correct Programs

The correct programs build up the mind and bring about an upward spiral for the individual. The best programs arise from inside the individual. The individual should know what they want, believe and desire it, and put forth the necessary action. In a sense, one can use their subconscious mind to bring about health, wealth, and prosperity. Since everything starts with the mind, one can "hack" their minds to bring about these things into their experience. When thoughts of health, wealth, and prosperity are so engrained into our subconscious that they become us, the conscious thought of it doesn't have to appear as much. You can focus on other things, be in the present moment and still attract health, wealth, prosperity. One can still spend time focusing on the thought, yet one shouldn't hold it for too long. Have the idea, combined with the other things listed, and let it go out into the universe and do its magic. When we hold onto thoughts, we block the flow of other things into our lives and make the manifestation process longer.

Programming happens every moment of the day. It can even occur in ways that we can't imagine nor see physically. As stated in a previous paragraph, you can either program yourself or be programmed. Even when one decides to program themselves, they will still have some programming from outside sources. When energy is built up, and one has a higher vibration, they will know the difference between the correct programs and the opposite. We must learn to control over minds.

With the overstimulation of today's culture, things like social media and television can be detrimental to the subconscious. A few seconds of seeing a picture on a timeline can create a slot in the mind. The effect continues to increase every time you see the image. One should do their best to be aware of that which they consume. I'd highly suggest for the avid social media users or TV watchers to unfollow pages detrimental to their success or well-being and follow what you would like manifest into your life. Create your own programs, use them wisely, and progress!

Making the Mind Your Friend

Do you want your mind to work with you or against you? I'm sure you would like your mind to work with you. It would be best if you had a healthy mind to make the mind your friend. We all have brains, yet how many of us use our minds? Thinking is an excellent activity if it is done in an organized, positive, and constructive manner. We must protect our mental.

A few primary ways to have a healthy mind and protect our mental is by:

- Diet. What are you consuming daily? This answer goes beyond food and what you taste. This deals with the senses as well. What are you watching? What are you listening to? Are you touching the "finer things" in life? Are you smelling good aromas? Are you seeing clearly and improving your vision of yourself and the world? A healthy diet gives us the fuel to perform better in many aspects of life and directly affects our thoughts. Everything we consume has a vibration, an energy field.

• Detoxing and fasting from certain things can be transformational and have a significant impact on one's life. These are ways to get the diet back in alignment. Listen to your spirit before and while partaking in the detoxification and fasting processes.

• Reprogramming. You will have to unlearn and relearn a lot of things that you know. It is imperative to let go of any beliefs, habits, notions, and any other items that no longer serve you. Reprogramming will require you to sacrifice. The process of reprogramming is not easy and will need lots of repetition, patience, and dedication. Actions yield results. The short-term pain has an equivalent success available for the long-term.

• Raising Your Vibration. With a higher vibration, life will become better, more joyful, and abundant. We must think in abundance to raise our vibration. Scarcity is the latter of abundance, yet with this comes limited thinking. We must know what we want out of life. Decisiveness helps us operate with purpose and opens us up to receiving those things we want out of life. Think and meditate on the things you enjoy doing, your values, your favorite dishes, etc. When you do things that align with you and bring you positive emotions, your vibration instantly rises. Living more in truth, harmony, balance, order, and love helps with this aspect.

• Activity. Be sure that you are utilizing your brainpower. Everything starts in the mind; therefore, an idle mind has a significant effect on life. To protect your mental, the necessary activity is required. Activities, along with the other things listed, boost brainpower. The higher your brainpower, the more easily you can live the life you want. Great ideas may come to you quickly, and you know how to control your thoughts. **Focus** is the foremost essential to activity. Focus is best achieved when you consciously know what you are doing. You are present in the moment. Reading, writing, and drawing are a few examples of activities. Activities are like the reps that lead to the sets in life. **Do activities that will protect your mental.**

CHAPTER 4: HEALTH IS WEALTH

To have a properly functioning vehicle, health must be a priority. Health plays a significant role in determining the direction of the mind, heart, body, and soul. Having good health will raise your vibration and lead you to that wealth energy. Wealth goes beyond an abundance of money; it can be an abundance of anything. One must take care of themselves to live the life that one wants.

Know Your Body

Splendid health first starts with knowing your body. All bodies are not the same. When knowledge of the body is acquired, you will know precisely how to build and maintain your body. The body must have great maintenance. The body must be taken care of and nurtured. Since everything is connected, if one thing isn't taken care of, effects can appear in other areas. Many health issues, especially physical ones, can be a manifestation of another thing. The cause can be major or minute. Many illnesses usually start in the soul first, then eventually transfers to the body.

Different cultures have explanations of body types. I resonate with the American philosophy of there being endomorph, ectomorph, and mesomorph. American philosopher William Herbert Sheldon created this classification system in 1940. Body types center mainly around genetics, yet they can change over time. Our DNA structure can give a blueprint to the natural look of our bodies.

The Three-Body Structure Types

Ectomorphs – Ectomorphs are naturally and effectively thin. They usually can eat whatever they want, without the weight being affected much. Ectomorphs are generally very athletic and active. Many ectomorphs may find it not easy to put on muscle mass or weight.

Endomorphs – Endomorphs find it easier to store fat and are naturally heavier. This body structure type is the opposite of ectomorphs. Endomorphs may find it not easy to lose weight and may have enormous appetites. They often have minimal muscle tone.

Mesomorphs – Mesomorphs are naturally "in shape." They usually find it easier to lose or gain weight, along with gaining muscle. Most mesomorphs have smaller appetites. This category is in between ectomorphs and endomorphs.

Knowing your bodily structure type isn't the only aspect of knowing your body. The three body types are only one factor. There are even Ayurvedic body types such as Vata, Pitta, and Kapha, which I suggest searching and reading.

The gut (core) is essential for the vehicles we are operating, our bodies. The gut comprises the intestines, stomach, spleen, liver, and colon, to name a few. It has even been considered for the gut to function as a second brain. If we are what we eat and then digest, then our consumption impacts our manifestations. Diet plays a significant role in having and maintaining a healthy gut. The gut feeling/ intuition is vital for knowing when to take action, making decisions, and even deciphering truths from lies. The core connects to our subconscious minds. When the gut is not in check, the willpower, clarity, and actions will not be in the best state. The gut is also connected with the Solar Plexus chakra, which is the third chakra. An imbalanced gut's physical manifestations include digestive issues, stomach ulcers, bloating, and abdominal pain. Pay attention when you feel the nudges and hunches within your core, and be aware of your health state.

When you know your body, you can better listen to your body. The effect of you listening to your body can be the difference between harmony and disharmony. In a harmonious state, the body can thrive.

A vital activity that a lot of people take for granted is rest. Getting the proper rest is a way to recharge, balance, and even heal yourself. The body will notify you when rest is needed. When the limits are pushed, our bodies go into overdrive and can lead to stress and increased levels of cortisol. Not everyone has to get the standard 7-8 hours of sleep. Your body will let you know when you've had little to no sleep, the right amount, or even overrested. The "taking no days off" thing is a big cliché, in my opinion. Rest is needed for proper performance and makes the building process more manageable.

Furthermore, when rest combines with the circadian rhythm, magic can happen. The circadian rhythm details the sleep-wake cycle and is a clock for our bodies. Melatonin, the sleep-regulating hormone is usually at its highest points around 10 pm-3 am. These are the best hours for deep sleep and when the body (mainly liver, lungs, and blood) repairs itself. Deep sleep is the best time for healing.

When you know your body, you can listen to your body, be aware of the signs, and know the proper actions to take. Specific diets are not for everyone. You can do research, trial-and-error, and get tests done, to name a few ways of knowing the proper diet for you. I believe that diet plays a significant role in lifestyle, muscle gain, and your overall vibration. Take great care of your temple, and your temple will take great care of you.

Activity and Brain Power

Activity is one of the main reasons for life and us being alive. With life, there is consistent motion and movement. Without movement, there would be death. I've already begun talking about the brain, and now I will discuss activity alongside this topic. Physical activity is the primary focus, and brainpower can be enhanced.

While we are alive, the body must move. Moving the body on a consistent basis can prolong our lives. This statement is not to say that we should move every second of the day. As stated in the previous section, you must know when to get your rest to become the best version of yourself. Moving the body gives us more energy. This can be from any activity, whether light, moderate, or heavy. Next time you experience any fatigue or a drop in energy, try stretching, going for a light walk or jog, do some pushups, etc., and watch how better you feel afterward. Morning to afternoon is the best time for activity, especially heavy activity. As humans, we are made to be active in the daytime. For those interested in losing weight, moving the body speeds up this process and makes you healthier.

With being active, the routine will be your best friend. Having a routine brings many benefits. What and how you do in one area of your life will translate to other areas of your life. I've noticed that having a routine has brought me benefits such as **strength, more consistency, enhanced discipline, and balance.** For those who are busy a lot or have heavy activity, a routine will take away some of the stress. Take the time, think consciously, and make a routine that best fits your lifestyle. Routine is not a one-size-fits-all approach; therefore, it is essential to know what works for you and suits your needs.

The fuel that enters our bodies has a direct impact on how we think and move. Fuel refers to anything that is consumed and energy. Food and content are significant factors when it comes to fuel. In the U.S., food and content are predominant. It is usually in the areas of food and content where things are exaggerated and overstimulated. Too much stimulation is not suitable for the senses and even the well-being of an individual. There are many fast-food restaurants in certain areas, food being advertised every second of the day, and many social media platforms. The more conscious you become, the more you will notice how many everyday things will not be best in excess. For instance, many fast-food restaurants use unhealthy oils, refined sugars, and fries a lot of their food. A diet full of fast-food will not sustain long-term and will lead to many issues. This topic also brings me to the subject of moderation. Everything should be consumed in moderation. Even the things that are good and the best can turn alarming when used in excess.

Knowing when to fuel is another essential factor. Being able to listen and tune into your body is necessary here. If someone were to eat at or around the same times every day, the body would become accustomed to eating around those times. If that person were to skip a meal and became hungry, they might not feel or perform at their best. Knowing when to fuel comes down to your personal preference and what works best for you. I suggest experimenting with different methods and times and seeing how your body reacts. Performing on an empty stomach is not always the best option. Having a light meal or snack, especially with healthy, nutritious foods that you favor, can make a difference. From personal experience, I've found that if I'm full from the night before and combine that with adequate rest, workouts in a fasted state are beneficial. Also, fasted workouts can, at times, give you more energy since the body isn't breaking down much food and using up a lot of your energy.

A few herbs, foods, and liquids that I recommend for brain power and activity are Ginkgo Biloba, fatty fish/ anything with omega-3 (ex. Walnuts, flax oil, salmon), Gotu Kola, Rosemary, Haritaki, Lion's Mane mushroom, green, leafy vegetables, herbal teas, berries, and water. Make sure to consult your health care practitioner or research before attempting anything you're unsure of and knowing what's suitable for your body.

What is A Diet?

A diet is a strategic plan that assists in creating a healthier and better lifestyle. Diets should center around the things that work best for you. Food isn't the only thing that makes up diets. I view diets as something that incorporates food, liquids, and other things that are consumed. Examples of other consumed things could include the energy you may receive, the music you listen to, and the environment. With creating and knowing the best diet, it is essential to listen. Listen to your body, mind, soul, spirit, and use your intuition. What works for one may not be necessary for another.

I've always heard people say that the Vegan diet is the best diet for every human being. I have to disagree and say that the best diet is what aligns with the individual. When it comes to food and hydration, if one pays attention to things such as their skin, digestion, thoughts, and performance, they can have an idea of what they might need. Some diets are meant to be short-term, and when we go beyond the period that our bodies can take the diet, problems may arise. Ensure that you get your macronutrients (calories, carbs, proteins, and fats) and your micronutrients (vitamins and minerals). These are essential, along with your amino acids.

Sugar is one of the main things that should be limited or, at best, avoided in diets. Natural sugars from sources such as fruits, honey, and maple syrup are better and can benefit. These still have to be in moderation. Added/ refined sugars are the worst forms of sugar. Too much sugar may lead to depression, fatigue, low motivation, bad breath, and low libido. Sugar, in excess, is also a sex killer. Drinking quality water, having a balanced lifestyle, herbs, and being active, are things that can outweigh the effects of sugar.

Oils are another factor that should be taken into mind when it comes to diet. Quality oils can supply quality fats. Oils can be used orally or applied externally, and used in recipes, to name a few. Fats help with the circulation in the body, cell growth and provides energy. Vegetable oils are unhealthy and, in large amounts, can clog up the arteries. They are usually cheap-produced oils that do not take into consideration the health of the consumers. These types of oils are usually found in baked goods/pastries, fast-food, and junk food products. Do your best to stay away from or highly limit vegetable, canola, soybean, cottonseed, and rapeseed oils. Oils such as coconut, grapeseed, avocado, sesame, and hemp oils are good for overall health.

The quality of your water is paramount. As humans, we are made of up to 70% water. Water has many properties and can transport nutrients, minerals, and vitamins throughout our bodies. Water allows the energy to flow. Water can cleanse and get rid of toxins in our bodies. Not all water is equal. Some water does not absorb appropriately upon consumption. The improper absorption of water is why some individuals may feel dehydrated, even after drinking the right amount of water. Tap water is the worst form of water. Most tap water may have waste or fluoride. Fluoride is an unhealthy substance that clouds the mind and disrupts the natural flow through the body. Some plastic bottled water may have BPA within, which is harmful. BPA or Bisphenol A is an industrial chemical used to make certain plastics. BPA exposure has been connected with many health problems, which I will not discuss in this chapter.

Tips for Overall Health & Well-being

- Stay hydrated and drink plenty of water.
- Use fluoride-free toothpaste and oral care products.
- Go for quality over quantity.
- Listen to your body and intuition.
- Get adequate rest.
- Maintain balance.
- Control and be aware of your breathing. Slow, deep breaths are the best. Shallow breathing depletes energy over time.
- Uplift and encourage yourself. Love yourself for who you are now and stay optimistic.
- Moderation.
- Limit screen time and use of electronic devices. Blue-light glasses are good to use if you need to be in front of a screen for long periods and support eye health.
- Get sunlight when possible. That Vitamin D is the truth! Spend time in nature and connect to the Earth.
- Be kind, generous, and live your truth.
- Take things day by day. Rushing and forcing things is not the best option. Patience is a virtue and may even bring great things and opportunities that you didn't imagine.
- Do things you love and enjoy.
- A healthy diet adds to overall well-being and progression. Take care of your health, and acquire that wealth, internally and externally.

CHAPTER 5: THE DIVINE WITHIN

Divinity is one of the many gifts from God. It is our God-given right to access the divine within. Many distractions in this modern world send many individuals drifting away from this remarkable phenomenon. We all have access to our higher selves and greatness. To access divinity, one must take the initiative and decide to take the path towards divinity. We are made in God's image; therefore, we can exhibit qualities of godliness. As stated in a previous chapter, we are spiritual beings having a human experience.

When one knows their spirit, they see the majority of who they indeed are. One gains more knowledge of their energy, powers, skills, abilities when they are in tune spiritually, have balance, and vibrate at a high frequency. The skin, flesh, your name, material possessions do not make who you are. As stated in "Know Thyself," we all have a specific blueprint we should adhere to that returns us to our natural state. The natural state is the highest. The divine within is like a master key. It may solve many problems, answer many questions, and can improve yourself and those around you.

Power, Purpose, & Spirituality

The word *power* refers to ability and strength. We all have power; we have to be aware of the power, have an intention for seeking it, and tap into our powers. Once we know our strengths, they can be used for good or evil. When power is used in the wrong way or falls into the wrong hands, things are not good. It's up to the individual to decide their path. Letting your power go to your head will only hold you back, as well as the misuse of power. Certain situations in life will reveal your power (s) to you. One should never give their power away. One should start by realizing the power that lies within them. Once the inner world is governed, the outer world becomes easier to understand and navigate.

In the mental and spiritual world, power doesn't determine consciousness. The physical world usually equates power to the material possessions accumulated, positions, rankings, and status. When the operator appropriately governs the mind and has a spirit-body connection, the soul awakens, and power generates similar to electricity. The soul is the intelligent aspect of man. The soul is like the match, and the spirit is the flame. The spirit is divine and sparks a flame that lights the match. The match has the fire and now brings light.

Along with power, the purpose is fundamental. Purpose is something you would do every day, even if you were not getting paid or financially compensated. There are many ways to profit from your purpose. Purpose can provide meaning to life and shouldn't be the only meaning. Life is beautiful; knowing and living your purpose can expose you to parts of the beauty. I'm not an expert on the many ways of profiting from purpose. There are many resources out there that provide an abundance of solutions. In the age of information that we live in, easier access to specific topics and fields is available.

Purpose is the thing that gives one energy, a feeling of being alive. Purpose can arise from the heart and be felt in the soul and spirit. Purpose and calling are very similar; I see them as cousins to each other. They both allow one to fulfill the mission that they were sent here to do. It's okay to feel your purpose is many things. I sometimes think this way, and I had to accept it. If you feel that your purpose is to do many things, think of one thing that ties it all together (ex. spreading divine love). If you are interested in being an expert in your field, having a purpose that you love/enjoy, and going with what you have an interest in excelling in while achieving your goals and adding value, make this easier.

Finding purpose is not always easy. It may take an extended period and many trials. Experimenting with various things, being adventurous, and asking for guidance has helped me get closer to my purpose. Purpose can be that one thing that you may have a strong feeling towards yet have been avoiding or may not have done in a while. In prayer, I usually thank God for guiding me towards my purpose. I also say, "God, please guide me towards my true purpose in life that I may add value and live my truth." Sometimes I may meditate, with my eyes closed (usually before bed), and ask, "What is my purpose? What was I sent here to do that I should fulfill? How can I add value for not only myself but to others and the world?"

When I write this book, I'm still searching for my true sol purpose, and I'm getting closer to my goal. While reflecting on purpose, I've learned how important it is. The reflection inspired me to include the importance of purpose in this book. A purpose-filled life leads to a happier life.

When it comes to religion and spirituality, there is always confusion between the two. There is a common misconception that to be spiritual; religion has to be involved. Some religious people may not be spiritual and spiritual people who may not be religious. Religion and spirituality are two sides of the same coin. Spirituality starts with the individual, while religion is an organized belief system. Both practices have similar aspects, including ethics, values, progression, and truth. Spirituality gives a unique edge because one can have the experience and find the pieces to put together the puzzle. I advise the individual who is reading this book to reflect on their level of spirituality or religion. Spiritual growth and knowing what resonates with you are likely to be ongoing, and the answers will eventually be revealed to you.

Some things may have been planted into us from external sources from a young age, and we may have never questioned these things. For me, the topic of religion and spirituality is an example. We need to know the how, why, and what of the things that we participate in. We are spiritual beings having a human experience. The spiritual part of us always seeks truth and deeper meanings to the day-to-day lives that we live. When the spiritual aspects are evolving, our energy grows with this part in a beautiful mixture.

There are spiritual laws that, when adhered to, will lead to success in many areas of life. Spiritual laws can be defined as innate codes. When applied correctly, we can live wisely. These laws involve the Universe and explain why things occur. Spiritual laws bring governance and balance many functions within the ever-changing world. Without a system that provides order, things will be chaotic.

Nature is the best example of spiritual law. If a tomato is planted, the result will be a tomato. What ye reap, ye will sow. Spiritual laws are definite in the way that they work. Spiritual laws are natural. If you look at nature, you can find many divine truths and connections to life. We are directly connected to nature. The phrase "Going with the flow" comes from nature and encourages us to not worry about things we have no control over. The wind moves swiftly and can change speed. I'm sure that there is an infinite number of spiritual laws. Below I'll list and discuss a few of the many spiritual laws.

1 The Law of Mentalism – All is mind. The Universe is mental.
2 The Law of Non-Resistance – Move in the direction of that which you want. There's no need to work over that which you don't want.
3 The Law of Correspondence – As above, so below. As below, so above.
4 The Law of Cause & Effect – Every cause has an effect. Every effect has a cause.
5 The Law of Vibration – Everything moves, everything vibrates. Nothing is entirely still.
6 The Law of Increase – That which you give thanks for will be multiplied.
7 The Law of Attraction – Your expectations have an effect on that which you'll receive. Where energy goes, energy flows.

8 The Law of Receiving – Give and ye shall receive. Be purposeful, have good intentions with your giving. The less you expect upon giving, the more you'll receive.
9 The Law of Forgiveness – Forgive yourself and others. In turn, you'll be forgiven.
10 The Law of Sacrifice – To get what we want out of life, some sacrifice must occur. Something has to be given up for the greater good. Everything has a price, and nothing is free.

Creativity & Divinity

If there is one quality that I would say is truly a gift once discovered, I would have to choose creativity. Creativity brings a sense of originality, balance, and freedom. Creativity is something that has no limits or boundaries set in place. It is a way of expression that can reflect in other areas of life. Creativity frees the heart, body, mind, soul, and spirit. I feel that creativity quickly connects one to the divine that is within.

The more something cultivates, the more that thing grows. Creativity unlocks new doors, avenues, and opportunities for you. The trailblazers and trendsetters of the world have some creativity. We all have creativity within. Some people have had a high level of creativity naturally from birth, while others have to find what brings out creativity.

Creativity can show you who you indeed are. Being creative raises your frequency. The first step with cultivating your creativity is being open to the energy. You have to want to be creative and have the intention. It would be best if you let the creative juices flow. There are certain days and times where creativity can be higher for a person or a collective. When the energy is great and high, creativity is at an all-time high. It's possible to transform negative energy into positive energy by being creative.

I believe that we all have an inner child. The inner child is the part of us that can see more joy in the world and enjoy life without taking it too seriously. We were all children at a part in our lives. The inner child stays with us and wants to be loved, acknowledged, and nurtured by us. The inner child is usually not recognized by many people in this fast-paced society. Stress is a primary factor that leads individuals to block their inner child and causes many unsatisfactory conditions. Childhood trauma is the immediate blockage after stress. When the inner child is activated, one can experience more youthfulness. Part of our nature is to have that "child-like" feeling and embrace the journey of life, which each thing being worthy of embracing and even bringing a sense of adventure. They may be more carefree and truthful. The inner child makes the world your canvas, and you learn to see the beauty in things and boost creative power.

If you may not feel your best, being creative can put you in a good mood and a better state of mind. Being relaxed and having good vibes can activate an outstanding level of creative energy. This is the kind that seems to put you into a flow state and experience bliss. Do what you find necessary or best to allow the creative energy to flow through you into your creation. I use music, deep breathing, and good scents when I need to set the mood for this creativity. In the next section, I will include how creative energy and sexual energy are inner-connected.

Sexual Energy

S.E.X. or Sacred Energy Exchange is one of the most potent energies out there. Sexual energy connects with creative and spiritual energy. They are all the same. In a hypersexualized society, it's essential to know the proper basis and profound meanings of sex. The higher groups in society see the power that sex has. The is why the topic is misrepresented in mainstream media. Improper education on sex can lead to misunderstandings regarding intimacy and other aspects of life. With the right knowledge and inner-standing of sex, it can transform your life.

The more sexual energy you have, the more you can tap into the divine within. Everything in the Universe is sex. Life force (ex. Earth) is feminine, and consciousness is masculine. Creation is all around us. Sex even occurs within our bodies with the cell processes. Cells can be created, regenerated, etc. When life is seen as sex, pleasure can be found even in simple things. Pleasure is a high vibration, and when it is combined with love (the heart) and true intentions, this is where major transformation can occur. As a healer or alchemist, you're able to turn pain into pleasure, hate into love, and many more.

Transforming and transmuting sexual energy assists with evolution and development. Sexual transmutation is using your sexual energy for a greater useful/purpose. Sexual energy is applied to another source (ex. Writing a book, going in nature). Sexual transmutation may appear in creative or practical expressions. Many great men and leaders use this method to achieve the things they want in life. One may become more driven or disciplined since one can harness one of the most potent energies. When a person is sexually disciplined, they tap into their power and become stronger. With sexual transmutation and many things in life, one must have the right intentions. The intent determines the actions and outcomes.

Semen retention separates orgasm from ejaculation. We are usually programmed to believe that ejaculation equals orgasm when the two are different. Semen retention truly is being able to orgasm without ejaculation. It builds up that arousal, letting it flow through the body and transmute that energy for a great purpose- which shows the connection between semen retention and sexual transmutation. Semen retention can be practiced while being celibate, yet the full effects come from orgasm without ejaculation. Limiting and withholding ejaculation will come naturally along the process. After sex, both partners should feel energized and better. Semen is man's vital life force and energetic code. Semen contains a plethora of vitamins and nutrients, such as Zinc, Magnesium, and Potassium. When man's semen is retained, the life force evolves, and man can have a more fantastic experience along this journey. Ejaculation is natural and should be limited or avoided. Yet, in the case of one, remedies such as rest, exercise, meditation, nutrient-dense foods (esp. Zinc, Vitamin D), and herbs (ex. Moringa, Sea Moss) are suitable for getting your energy up. If Semen Retention becomes a lifestyle for a man, he can live a better life. Semen Retention is only a start and should not be seen as the one-all.

Sex should be done with intention and should be an act that is enjoyed. When choosing your partners, choose them wisely. Energy is being exchanged during sex. You are taking part of another being's vibration with you during the activity. Get to know the person before you all have intercourse. Sex can be used to heal when the right intentions are applied. Orgasms are natural, and everyone deserves them. They can make one see the beauty in life, get rid of trauma, experience bliss, ecstasy, and the high vibration of love. Living an orgasmic reality can help you see the good in many things while also seeing the truth.

Sex magic is using sexual energy to manifest hopes, dreams, goals, or desires. It encompasses focus and visualization on that which is desired. One has to have the intention and visualize while doing sexual activity. This intention and visualization duo can be done solo or with a partner. With a partner, if both individuals focus on and imagine the same thing at once, this energy increases and amplifies, speeding up the results and time that it takes to manifest. I suggest before having conscious sex to meditate, know, and connect with your partner. Ask and share goals and dreams. If you all trust each other and love each other, the sex will be unique.

Porn is something that we as evolved ones should significantly limit and eliminate. Some evil entities are found within some videos and have a parasitic effect. The media that is portrayed today on various sites are bizarre, overstimulating, and addictive. The content is made this way because the elite knows the brain's powers and how when porn is used as a substance, it can lead to many problems for a person. Watching porn causes dopamine to skyrocket at a horrendous rate unnaturally. It is also easy to cause addiction. Long-term use of porn may negatively impact the brain's neurons and cause one to have a weird view when it comes to sex. Porn-induced E.D. and Premature Ejaculation are common problems amongst men who use it long-term. Some ways to overcome these issues are through:

- Breathing Exercises. Qi-Gong/ Tai' Chi, Yoga.
  - Ab Breath and breathing through from the stomach comes in. Start by inhaling through the nose. You'll notice that the belly expands outwards. Then exhale, noting that the stomach comes back in. The exhale can be performed through the mouth or nose, whichever is comfortable for the person. Putting your hand on your tummy can help as well. Doing the Ab Breath for a few minutes can increase mood and welcome more positive energy.
  - Qi Gong/ Tai' Chi/ Yoga is good for the mind, body, and spirit. These exercises get the energy flowing throughout your body and also can focus on the breath.
- Herbal Remedies
- Interacting with women. Smiling and being genuine when in contact with a woman.
- Going into nature and grounding. (Planting feet on the Earth. Barefoot in soil, grass, or sand is best.)
- The Deer Exercise (for men and women)
- Kegels and Reverse Kegels

Sexual attraction occurs by polarities. Polarity is two sides of the same coin. Masculine (yang) and feminine (yin) are the two polarities in this instance. When one being has their feminine more online, and the other has their masculine more online, this is where the highest level of sexual attraction forms. Opposite poles attract. Polarity can also be viewed and understood in terms of a car battery (the effects of negative and positive). A negative pole and positive brings that power generation. If there were two negative poles or two positive poles, the charges would repel each other. We all have masculine and feminine energies within us, and these energies must be cultivated and balanced for us to have a great experience along this journey.

CHAPTER 6: BUILDING THE RIGHT CIRCLE

The things that one associates with, activities that are habitually partaken in, and surrounds themselves with over some time will become a part of one's vibration. Energy is found in everything, especially with the individuals whom one is around. Influence plays a massive factor in terms of our life's trajectory. We can either stay the same, grow upwards, or spiral in the latter of upwards. In-fluence, which breaks down to "in-flow," should begin with God, the spirit, the divine forces, and yourself. This higher vibration then works through a person's character or destiny and goes beyond daily life. Influence can turn into a legacy. When people are influenced by the wrong sources, people, etc., value is not being added, and there is an energetic shift in a direction that is usually not desired deeply.

When it comes to people and building the right circle, one must love God and themselves first to fully maximize the experience with their relationships, partnerships, life, the outside world, and other people. Perception does matter. How you see yourself is likely how you view others. Harmonious relationships are where there is a connection, and harmony brings balance and uplift. There is an agreeance; both sides find value and synchronize- which does not mean that all harmonious relationships are perfect. Like any regular relationship, there are ups and downs, yet values such as harmony, truth, and love exist in the long-run. Harmony should be taken into account when building the right circle.

The right circle welcomes and embodies harmonious relationships, along with a significant elevation. A circle symbolizes unity. When two or more circles come together, despite their differences, there is still unity and commonalities.

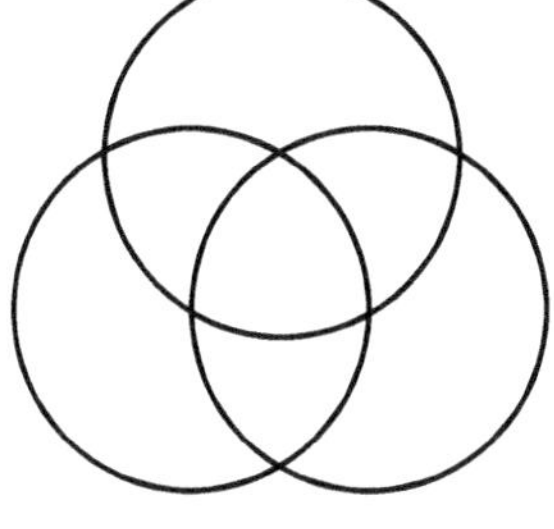

Venn Diagram

Perfect Match

The word "perfect" comes in many forms and has many definitions for many people. I believe that there are many great and highly efficient matches. Perfection, in reality, still has some flaws. The output of a perfect input (s) is made with quality in mind. Quality is the precursor to success. The perfect match encompasses unity, love, and devotion at its highest level. In this situation, both individuals have a deep connection to each other. Together they are an unstoppable and powerful force. It's almost as if the two auras blend and create one giant field. They always support and are there for each other.

Perfect is what the person makes it. For example, if someone views perfection as love and happiness, they may strive towards it. While love and happiness may not always be present, this person may have these qualities and consider those on the level of love and happiness to be a good fit for them. This person will usually find themselves resonating with those on a similar path. The qualities you wish for others to have must already be within you or qualities you are striving towards, even if they are not fully developed. Build your inner circle first, then your outer circle. Over time, both will successfully build simultaneously.

One shouldn't rely on others and external sources all the time for their happiness. Relying solely on external sources can lead to dependency. Dependency creates stagnation towards happiness. Happiness is a divine right, and when genuine, can lead to those that are for you. The perfect match, as they may call it. Happiness should start from within. Escapism, running away from problems, not acknowledging or feeling your emotions, and how you're genuinely feeling are a few examples of blockages to complete happiness.

Ways to overcome the tendency of "perfectionism" are understanding, having an open mind, and being realistic. There can sometimes be this attachment with perfectionism and can cause innumerable expectations to come into play. Thus, if the situation doesn't work out perfectly, this may cause disappointment in the individual. Perfectionism puts pressure on the individual, that when the pressure is exaggerated for too long can cause disharmony. Everything will not turn out perfect, and it's a part of life. You should always be able to expect the best and know that good comes out of every situation.

Relationships are the state of being related. I've listed good relationships by a few qualities, and I'll share my view on good relationships as a whole. Good relationships nourish the mind, body, soul, heart, and spirit. Both sides give and receive value. Most importantly, they add mutually to each other. Good relationships bring the individuals to be more in tune. The individuals' love, appreciate, respect, and attempt to know each other better. A good relationship doesn't have to be a match made in heaven; it can only be as one view and makes the relationship.

One should have standards, know what they want, what they can add, and what they are looking to gain before relationships, especially those intimate. Relationships can also be viewed as a business. If you're the person who owns a company, wouldn't you be looking for partners or other individuals among whom you can expand? The boundaries should be set clear while the relationship is present, and both sides should know. It's okay to go with the flow. Forcing things can bring more resistance. Go into relationships and anything in life with good intentions, and you'll receive good.

Be the light, and you're a step ahead towards attracting the right people to you.

Your Vibe is Your Tribe

The energy that you put out is what you'll receive. This statement is a spiritual law. To receive, you must give. Giving doesn't just tie to money; it can also relate to your time, presence, energy, even a smile or encouraging words. Giving is the thing that makes one open and deserving to receive.

Even if you may not know or associate, the people you encounter can reflect you somehow. We can see in others what we see in ourselves. As human beings, we are not entirely the same, yet we have more in common than we think. Those who you may see more similar or, at times, the piece to a puzzle is usually those people call friends, homies, etc. If you are not satisfied with what you are receiving, in this the people you naturally attract, change must happen.

The subconscious mind can be a factor in the people, places, experiences, and situations that one attracts. Some memories and external thoughts may have been deeply planted into the subconscious mind that needs to be addressed. When specific issues (ex. Heartbreak, not forgiving someone) are not addressed, they may sit in the subconscious, limit perception, and replay. Remember that repetition is the key to change. When it comes to the subconscious mind, positive thoughts, actions, good intentions, programming, surrounding oneself with beauty are a few things that can enhance what one receives, even if it may seem minute.

- Start by being true to yourself and see that light within; let it shine. You are great.
- Love yourself. Be disciplined.
- Know what you want.
- Heal thyself first.
- Show gratitude and be thankful.
- Go to environments that allow you to be you, that you are likely to meet like-minded individuals.
- Tell the truth and be genuine.
- Listen
- Experiment and get outside of your comfort zone.
- Be who you would want to surround yourself with.
- Collaboration over competition.

The Circle Criteria

When it comes to building the right circle, there must be criteria involved. The criteria are equivalent to the structure of a building. It provides grounding and is the substance that can make or break relationships or the circle. The values are where the actual foundation of the circle can be found.

What do you and those apart of the circle value? Are there any similar values? How can we build upon these values?

A few of the values I believe in are truth, love, loyalty, respect, and appreciation.

The circle should feel like a safe haven for you to be who you are and express your truth. Great circles almost feel like family and energize you while with the people and after an interaction. They have you feeling motivated, creative, and better.

When building a circle, one must know what they are looking for in others and what they can bring to the table.

The criteria should be dependent on the needs of the person and the circle. The standard has to be mutual for the circle to be sustainable and efficient in the long-term. If a circle is short-term, there still needs to be a clear understanding of everyone within that circle, and values, goals, and expectations must even be put in place and adhered to. If the needs don't agree with both parties, a resolution can be acquired. The resolution will require communication, lots of listening, respect, open-mindedness/ adaptability, and reasoning.

Intuition is a powerful tool that is beneficial for circle building. It is the inner voice and knowing that comes without a conscious need. It is also known as a hunch, gut feeling, and the sixth sense. The intuition must be built and trusted by the individual. It may not always be right, yet intuition can give one discernment and aids in decision-making. If you are an intuitive or a natural feeler, then you know almost automatically if something is right or not right. We can feel the energy of things and others. If the energy is off, your intuition usually may send a warning, or you may get an unusual feeling. Intuition can guide one towards building and being a part of the right circles.

CHAPTER 7: OVERCOMING ADVERSITIES

Adversity is defined as a condition of misfortune, hardship, difficulty, or distress. These are times when the towel is more likely to be thrown in or when many may feel misguided or not feel encouraged. Hard times are only temporary. They can sometimes be a test or a moment that can make one stronger. Hard times can be a gift to prepare one for more prominent and great opportunities in the future. These times may reveal dormant abilities and ways to use these abilities. The way that one views the situation and the actions taken plays a significant role in the outcome. Times of adversity are usually considerable learning experiences and can even be a spiritual awakening.

During the recent year of 2020, there was a major shift in the world. I believe that many people came to know more about who they are. Many opportunities, businesses, and platforms were created. I've seen unity grow, and while social distancing Is a thing, people found new ways to communicate. The truth revealed itself, giving that 2020 vision. More people found ways to overcome adversity.

Strength, growth, and mindset are three main factors when it comes to overcoming adversity. The sections ahead in this chapter will reveal why and include many other factors.

The Plan

The first step in overcoming adversity is being aware of your situation, then coming up with solutions. I like to call this "The Plan." Planning is essential because it allows one to become more organized, the reason for the actions taken, and tremendous success in the near future. Greater success is likely to be achieved because the planning may even bring goals within the process. One may tap into their desires and the things that they want to achieve. Planning gets one closer to the desired result. The plan gives one direction.

While planning is beneficial, one should learn how to go with the flow and not force things. When things are forced, there is still resistance present. Resistance does not lead in the right direction and can sometimes be a distraction from the prize. Changing plans is the step needed when the current plan is not working. Being adaptable and welcoming change is a part of going with the flow. Sometimes plans need to be made on the fly. Some moments may require planning. One should give the plan time and develop it prior to action for the best results. When plans are forced, they don't receive the proper development.

When planning, if one doesn't know what to do, asking their intuition is beneficial, and being patient and reflecting before action. The intuition can hold and reveal many answers if it is trusted.

Prayer and guidance are beneficial in planning. When one prays, they allow for guidance in the desired direction. Prayer is useful for the nervous system. It instantly raises one to a theta state, which is of a higher vibration. It's essential to be thankful and have faith when praying to do so with the right intent. Ask for guidance to go in the right direction. When rightly applied, prayer can be life-changing and powerful. When praying, energy is being sent out to the universe. When the vibrations of words and thoughts are sent out, one should let them go and continue living life. Holding them will bring resistance.

When creating The Plan, know that even a single idea can go far. Many ideas start with one idea. The process can be precious in itself. The thought and effort of ideas count as well. Take time to think through ideas to use in the plan(s). Ideas can come at random times. I find that the most ideas come when I'm able to relax and become calm.

You should always prepare and expect the best. The Law of Attraction states: "That which you expect, you receive." While this is only part of the law, the way you prepare plays a significant role. There are many ways to prepare for the best. It starts with faith, having optimism, and knowing what you want. The journey in itself is a learning experience, so be prepared to learn and evolve.

Long-term satisfaction over short-term gratification works many wonders. When choosing this route, they have the future in mind and don't let adversity stop them. They instead use the situation as a building block and keep moving.

Making Peace with the Situation

To make peace with a situation is empowering. The situation can be seen without discrimination. Discriminating a situation can cause a limited perception and doesn't add value. If one has a positive approach and mindset to a situation, one can grasp some positive factors. Every "failure" holds the seed of an equivalent success. It all comes down to what one makes of the situation. Being optimistic can boost mood, creativity, drive, and results.

Making peace with a situation allows for one to gain more knowledge and wisdom. Since the peace factor strengthens the inner, one can become more resilient. The inner can become calmer and process things better when peace forms. One can take the facts, learn, and apply the knowledge via the situation. Learning from and making peace with situations give insight into the future and similar situations. While all situations are not the same, many lessons will hold for most situations. While everyone may have similar situations, we may have unique experiences regarding the detail and analysis of the situation.

Change and opportunity can arise from making peace with a situation. Peace is a high vibration that can open many doors. Peace brings along with its balance. Balance is the optimal way of life. When things are balanced, they are healthy. Every situation, especially that of adversity, can bring with it change. Change is a sign of evolution, and when we evolve, we grow and become stronger. One should intend to change for the better and seek truth in what they do and how they live. The mind can be used to generate opportunities and ways to create new adventures.

Remember to love and believe in yourself, especially during these times. Take good care of yourself and your health. Make sure that you're good before helping others. When giving during times of adversity, it's still best to provide genuinely when you do give. Whether it's your energy, a compliment, a service, money, give genuinely and with good intention, and you'll receive. Stay strong and well.

When you believe in yourself, you send out a sign to the universe that you are deserving, and you instantly raise your vibration.

Show love to people, love your neighbors and be thankful. A little support, even in a subtle way, can be memorable. Sometimes what may seem a simple action to you may be life-changing for another. Always be mindful of this. Actions speak louder than words.

The Divergence Factor

The Divergence Factor is the foremost step that impacts the outcome and advancement. It separates being in the same situation from being in a better position. The Divergence Factor is about taking action. Action is the effort that is applied. Any effort that is applied will bring forth results. The frequency that one uses the actions, the planning, and intention all affect the outcome.

Perseverance, along with the action, makes for a great road ahead. I define persisting as putting in continuous effort despite obstacles. It is not giving up at that which is desired. Perseverance is when one doesn't resist that which they don't want. They know what they want and work towards that. It gives guidance and direction.

A change of plans is usually needed when: the current plan isn't working after various attempts or a realization/ change of direction has occurred. There can be times when it seems no matter what action has been taken; the plan isn't making progress. Some plans take longer to develop and work compared to others.

Having a vision or plan prior to taking action yields the best results. The vision gives one a structure. This structure leads to efficient decision-making, therefore, better action.

Believing in yourself and being open and deserving for the significant change gives many advantages. When you believe in yourself, you also prove that you believe in the divine forces and the universe. The divine forces and the universe want you to trust them and believe in yourself. Having faith adds a positive influence on the outcome. To have a feeling of openness and deserving, one should prepare to receive. Whether its actions such as a diet change, more exercising, or moving locations, one should intend to change for better reasons. This goes directly with faith and proving that you trust the universe.

One must build discipline and know how to control themselves. Self-control is about knowing your shadow side and the things that must be managed to ensure your growth. The shadow side, when untamed, can lead to negative manifestations, i.e., anxiety, depression. I view the shadow side as a wild lion that must be tamed. When first coming into contact with the shadow side, it may roar; it may be overwhelming. Over time, one will learn how to control the shadow side, control themselves, and continue to grow in all areas. What's done in one area affects the other areas. Everything is connected. Start by examining habits, patterns, thoughts, actions, and reflect on those which don't serve you and make the change. Some individuals can completely cut bad habits, while it's a longer process for others. Try what works best for you.

Every situation is a learning experience. Use every situation to make you better.

CHAPTER 8: GIVING VALUE

What is value? Value is the merit and importance of something. Value goes beyond money, status, and positions. In this world, nothing is free since even the free things have a "price" attached to them of some kind, whether it's time, involvement, or energy. When something is of high value, it is held in high regard. If a person is of high value, they usually take good care of themselves, know who they are, have principles, values, and a great character.

Popularity and riches are not the things that solely determine a high-value person. Many individuals are high-value and may not be popular or have the most money. They usually have a level of freedom, confidence and think well of themselves. When one thinks well of themselves, this causes others to believe well of them subconsciously.

People can provide value in innumerable ways. Knowing the best ways that one provides value can enhance their creative force and improve their life. Think of ways that you provide value, and you may generate ideas towards your purpose.

Know Your Worth

When it comes to value, it's essential to know your worth. Worth is what one believes they deserve and describes the value that is placed on something. The first step of knowing your worth is knowing who you truly are. Knowing who you truly are, take into account your gifts, talents, skills, and abilities. We all come to this lifetime with natural gifts, skills, talents, skills, and abilities granted to us by the divine forces. If we tap into and cultivate these gifts, we raise our vibration, feel more in tune and move towards our soul's purpose. We all have the choice and can acquire many skills and abilities through this life experience.

The more that you know, use and grow, the higher your value continues to rise. Knowing your worth will guide you towards the right path. When I doubt my worth, I've noticed how I wasn't living up to my potential. Others would pick up on this frequency, and I would always know there's more. Believe in yourself, know your worth, do things out of good intention, and you already step ahead in succeeding with what you do.

When you are living and moving in your purpose, the money will come to you. I always remember my elders tell me, "Don't chase the money; let the money chase you." I truly understand this now due to experience. It's best to cultivate your craft and the things you are good at it. When you love what you do, this sends out a frequency to the Universe, giving you a high possibility to profit from what you are doing and continuing to grow. When you're living more in your truth, have discipline, put in the action, having the intention to grow, and other beneficial qualities, you'll notice how easy money comes to you. It may seem magical, yet it is, in fact, natural due to the Laws of Nature.

Money isn't the only thing that determines worth. There are many other factors such as influence, quality, and service to take into account. Money is an energy. We still have to have good energy towards money. When money has good energy towards it, sound energy returns via this currency to the individual. Money itself isn't the root of all evil. Love and obsession for it is. The love of money manifests when it's the only focus of an individual. There's infinite supply in this Universe. Money wasn't made to be hoarded. Give, save, spend, and invest, and do so wisely.

When your worth is known, you know what you bring to the world and can share these great gifts. Knowing your worth can instantly be uplifting for the spirit. When you know your worth and tap into your truth, your intuition can become your best friend. Not only can having a great intuition help you in business/career decisions, but it can also help you in other areas of your life. Intuition can be the key that can guide you towards the door that is right for you. Sometimes we may not get the message correct, yet with experience, we learn to trust that "gut feeling." Your intuition can guide you where you need to go. It is usually God, the source, divine forces, spirit guides, or ancestors giving one the messages. It's essential to develop intuition and trust it.

Go where you are loved and appreciated. When you're in positive environments, you're likely to excel and uplift yourself and others at the same time. When you know your worth, you refuse to settle for less than you know you deserve and be around negative energy. When one goes where they are loved and appreciated, they can easily enjoy their job.

Knowing your worth is the merit one places on themselves regardless of outside influence. This person knows what's best for them, how to move efficiently, provide quality, and be of service.

"When you know your worth, no one can make you feel worthless." – Anonymous.

Value Consciousness

When value meets consciousness, the result is Value Consciousness. Consciousness is when one has a state of awareness. Value consciousness is being aware of the value in yourself and the things that are around you. It can also see the good in things, for even bad situations or mistakes can carry an equivalent or greater good.

Value consciousness is about the mindset. This state requires the individual to focus more on the abundance and positive aspects. Value consciousness means that the energy is focused on that which is beneficial. In value consciousness, perseverance and patience go a long way. You can do something despite the roadblocks, using your roadblocks as stepping stones, having faith, and enduring despite the difficulties.

Taking the extra mile can bring more than one may have expected in the long term. This route sparks enthusiasm in the individual and shows their faith in the Laws of Nature. Taking the extra mile can bring out the best in one and reveal the purpose behind their actions.

All effort counts, no matter if one may feel otherwise. Even if the effort isn't received, rewarded, or acknowledged by another source, eventually, one will be rewarded in some way by the Universe. All the effort that one applies makes them stronger and cultivates their skills. It's like finishing a project. The idea or plan is created, the action follows, and the schedule can be created based on the creators and other factors, such as deadlines and due dates. God, The Universe, and divine forces are always watching and see your efforts. When one helps themselves, great things are destined to come their way.

Giving value uplifts the collective. Society as a whole benefit from value. You never know how far a word or action can go. There are words and actions that last a lifetime and can significantly impact a person or society as a whole. To the giver, it may be a small gesture. To the receiver, it could be very influential. One can find value every day in the little things that often go unappreciated by many. When value is seen in an unbiased way, the gates can be open for more value to flow.

Customer service can be a good example of value consciousness. The company usually puts their customers as a priority. Ensuring that the customers have a great experience, the company puts measures in place to stick to their mission and values and adequately serve their customers. When customers have a great, memorable, and unique experience, it forever sticks with them, and they are likely to be repeat customers.

In business, value consciousness can also reflect in knowing your target market. The target market is the group that your company/ product/ service is the most likely to appeal to. The target market is where the majority of the marketing efforts are applied. Categories such as gender and age are used to create the target market. Having a target market as a company reveals that the company is aware of their customers and is well-suited to assist their customers and be of service.

Value consciousness emphasizes quality and being of service. When things are done to the best of their ability, great results are yielded in the long term. Numbers have power as well, and quality can last for up to generations. Being of service means to provide without expectation. When one gives without expectation, they are calmer and can consistently improve with their efforts. Expectations set boundaries and can cause disappointment if things don't go the right way.

When one is of service, they care about people and have the right intentions while being of service. Being of service can change lives and make this world a better place—even efforts such as donating, giving advice, or being a volunteer fall under this category.

How to Apply Value

- Be conscious of the why and start with an intention. It's essential to have a sense of direction. It's okay to find direction while on the journey. Being definite with a plan and knowing your value makes navigating the journey more comfortable. We have to recognize that which we can control and not stress over that we cannot control. Sometimes we have to let things work their way.
- Have values and principles in place as a foundation for the value being given. Values and principles are the pillars that are stood on and stood for. If honesty is one of your pillars, apply this in your application, and stand by it. Provide your value with this honesty and watch the business grow. Decide on your values and principles and implement them into your life and applications.
- Know the things that you offer. Knowing what you offer helps you be conscious of your value and share your gifts with the world. Reflect on the things you're good at, whether natural or learned. I've found that making a list of these things helps. Ask people who know you well of the things they see you being good at.
- Provide the things that you offer with quality and love. Be appreciative of your gifts, talents, skills, and abilities. Use what you have to the best of your ability.
- Be of service and approach involved parties with love and genuineness. For example, if you're collaborating on a project or meeting a busi-

ness partner, imagine they are your brother or sister, and approach them with love and good energy while being genuine. Help each other grow and thrive.

- Create a price range (if for profit).
- Incorporate enthusiasm into what you do. The etymology (origin of a word) of enthusiasm means to be divinely inspired and guided by God. Incorporating this excellent quality into your application brings quick and consistent growth, and one can see the beauty in what they do and provide outstanding service.

CHAPTER 9: LEAVING YOUR MARK

Leaving your mark is about knowing what you want to leave here on this Earth plane. It is also about a contribution to the future. It's about being the best you and making this world a better place. We are all connected in some way, so what you do affects others. The world is like a mirror, where things are continually being reflected.

Energy never dies; it is only transferred and keeps moving. Life and death are polar opposites. Death can be considered as the beginning of life. Life has creation and destruction, which are polar opposites as well. To grow, one has to make some sacrifices, may experience a rebirth, and heal. The growth process gets one closer to leaving their mark in this world since it pushes one closer to their true purpose. When a mark is left in this world, the energy is prominent, and there's still existence in some form.

Leaving your mark goes directly with the truth. The more one is in alignment with truth and knows their purpose while here, the more likely they are to impact significantly. Even if a person doesn't care much about leaving their mark, energy still follows.

Game Time or Practice?

Leaving your mark is first about embracing your uniqueness and the person you are. No one individual is the same as another. There can be similarities, as seen with twins, yet varying aspects exist between the two. We all have a unique blueprint for this lifetime. A part of this blueprint lies our purpose, personality, and destiny.

When it comes to destiny, the free will and decision of the individual matter- destiny can be seen as a prediction of events or predetermined things. The ultimate decision is in the hands of God and the universe.

We are all sent here with a mission that has to be accomplished. When the mission is departed from, this may cause karma on one's future or the future of one's children. The decisions that we make impacts our life. One decision can change your life. We live in a world that operates on cause and effect. For every cause, there is an effect. If one does good, they are likely to continue attracting good. The majority of life is predetermined, while the rest is free-will and the decision of the individual.

Fulfilling your purpose is a way to fill the empty void. If you've ever wondered why even after successes, losses, gains, and thriving in the material world, some people still have an empty feeling inside, it is most likely due to a need to fulfill a purpose. Depending on external sources to fix an internal situation only goes so far. Getting to the root cause allows for long-term growth and fixing the problem once and for all. Fulfilling your purpose is internal, as much as it is external.

The lives we are living are present. Time exists in the material world, and nature doesn't know time. In this way, time can be considered an illusion. I believe that while we are here, time is a great asset and should be used wisely. A wise use, management, and application of time lead to great success. Time works better with us the more we are in alignment with our true self and love.

Love is essential since it is one of the highest vibrations, and when combined with time, it creates a balance and flow effect. When operating in love, the energy is amplified and can balance a situation, causing things to flow in a prosperous manner.

Enjoy life and be grateful for everything that you already have.

Things shouldn't be rushed. Patience allows things to fall into place at the right time when the necessary compensation is applied. If one is looking to advance, they should give good effort and intend to improve along with other good intentions. When a small space can no longer be occupied, it has no choice but to grow larger.

There's a possibility that everything can be happening at the same time from a larger perspective. From the outside looking in, we can focus on the synchronicities, patterns, details, truth, and things to improve. The inside looking out (inner self-examining the external world) can sometimes cause a focus on things that are not essential to our growth or may cause unnecessary judgments. When both perspectives are cultivated throughout the journey, one becomes stronger and can navigate life better. One may discern better, know how to plan and act wisely. These perspectives are essential to having an impact.

It's currently game time and no longer practice. When we live in the present, the game of life continues, and the player of the game (you) have the power to control the game and to play it wisely. The past was practice, and now it's time to continue building, be decisive and definite, continue thriving, control your thoughts, and take action. When you control this game, a.k.a. your reality positively, you're able to see its incredible effects and how if you believe something, you can see that thing. When you make the best out of what you have, the best will come to you—realizing that it's game time and giving it your best positively influences leaving your mark.

As many actions lead to equal and opposite reactions, so do the things you do, the person you are, etc., affect the world.

Innovation

Bringing advancement and moving things forward in this society creates a better present and prosperous future. Innovation brings out the best in the creators and the world at large. Things are continually advancing and moving forward, and the more some support innovation, the closer to unity we move. I see innovation as putting differences to the side, creating solutions for the problems, realizing the connection between everything, and improvement.

Innovation is about being the change in the world. It is acknowledging that light within you and letting it shine. We are all born with a light that is within us. When we discover and cultivate this light, we start to radiate, become more grounded, balanced, and enjoy the journey. When we care for and love humanity and ourselves, we move towards harmony. Think of all the great inventions that are out there. The inventor usually thought of a problem or need and created something that can move things forward. It all started with an idea. In this mental universe that we live in, the mind can assist us with innovation. Like minds are connected and can contribute to a significant change in the world with the right intentions, good planning, collaboration, and action.

When we are the change in the world, we inspire others to be the change in the world and advance towards and connect with their higher selves. We encourage others to live their truth and connect with their consciousness. This sound energy brings along an elevated shift in mankind. We are all leaders in some way. Different personalities, styles, and methods of leadership exist. Variety and diversity bring uniqueness. We have to know when to lead and when to follow. Every master has had to submit to some master to advance. Advancement does come with many tests, sacrifices, and moments to grow. The straight and narrow path is the best for innovation.

Standing for what you believe in is a form of innovation. When this belief is a form of truth (perfect harmony), its impact can be primary—standing for what you believe is an expression of faith. When it comes to this belief, whether it's via values, principles, actions, etc., one should know when to keep an open mind. Standing firm in that which is in harmony with God and the Universe brings many blessings to your life.

Innovation adds adventure to life and spices up things. Adventures add exploration and discovery to the things in life. Sometimes a trip to a foreign land, trying a new dish, and getting out in nature, for example, can invigorate new ideas. Stepping out of the old into the new can keep things flowing. With innovation, some risks have to be taken to advance. Sometimes the unknown can hold within it the greatest truths and beauty. If the unknown is not explored, how would we know it's there? Taking strategic risks and incorporating adventure into life can add to life and the world simultaneously.

Timeless art is an art that is remarkable and easy to remember. It stands out from the other pieces of work and has that unique vibe to it. This creation may bring great emotion. You recognize its beauty and feel moved after being in the presence of the creation. Timeless art is similar to a diamond in the rough. It keeps shining and can even uplift the things around it. Getting better with age and time and having a profound impact on creation is an area where timeless art excels and brings tremendous innovation to the world. This type of art withstands the face of time. Many artists, musicians, and other great souls have brought us timeless artwork, and we still can hear, see, and witness the greatness that these great souls have left here today.

Influencing the Next Generations

"Energy never dies. It is only created or transferred."

By leaving your mark, you are serving as an inspiration for others. The inspiration is usually distributed to those in the present and the ones who are the future. As time progress, each generation progresses. Each generation begets new life, ideas, creations, and infinite other marvelous aspects. Some of the elements from previous generations are carried to the current and later generations.

There is always the potential for new greatness to be produced.

The word "generation" also applies to the masculine and feminine forces. These are the giving and receiving forces, the active and passive. Within generation is creation.

Your presence on Earth at this time has an impact on the next generation. If you're an individual who likes to keep things moving forward, work with the natural laws, and operate in truth, I'm sure you'll have a great impact and leave a great legacy behind.

The word "afterlife" means future life. If the word is arranged in reverse order, it translates to life after. It is the life after the current life. When two forces come together and create one, they are connected. Firm connections on a spiritual level are potent.

Legacies have cycles, which can be continued or altered. Some individuals may come to this world to be the change that their family or society needs. This process is a breaking of a cycle to form a new one. The new cycle has its foundations on the previous cycle, which provides a form of stability. People who are meant to alter a cycle may feel a need to fulfill a higher purpose that is greater than them or may feel unique, ubiquitous, or like they're not in the right place. In actuality, you are in the right place, and there's a reason for everyone's existence.

Knowledge of how to leave a mark is essential. Every cause has an effect, and for every action, there is a reaction. We are all bodies, a part of one general body. Even the small steps we take affects the health of the general body. When you think of the human body, many systems work together to operate the body. Our mark is a part of the world's footprint. What if the body of the world is the real "Bigfoot?"

A few ways that many individuals have left their marks are through creative expressions (ex. art, music, literature), family/children, organizations, companies, inventions, and products, promoting truth, and advocating for advancement.

The above list is only a few examples of leaving a mark. There are many ways to have a significant, memorable impact on the world. It is up for you, the reader, to decide how you will leave your mark and help cultivate the world and future.

SUMMARY

When you realize your true power and light, you'll be amazed at many of the things which happen in your life. Some may seem magical or supernatural. What you believe you can see.

Remember to use your mind wisely in this mental university, in this game we call life. Everything is mental. Your thoughts and attitude determine reality. We are creators of our reality, and if there's an undesirable situation, you have the power to change that into something better. Emotions with thought and repetition make manifestation quicker. Focus on that which you want while blessing the obstacles and the undesirable. Your perception determines your reception. Start thinking positive, uplifting thoughts.

Life is in everything; everything has consciousness and energy. Sex is life. There is creation, destruction, and transference.

Love yourself and have a love for all. Love is the highest vibration and has the power to heal. It is a powerful yet sensitive force. Divine love combines tolerance and peace. What we wish for others, we want to unto ourselves.

We are made in God's image. We are expressions of the creator. Trust the divine forces and the universe.

The universe is one song. Sound is truth and harmony. The higher your frequency, the more in tune you are.

Have pure faith and believe that whatever happens will be good. Expect the best for yourself and humanity. Let go of any limiting beliefs, thoughts, actions, and habits. Believe in yourself. Let your light shine; stop fearing your light.

Remember to embrace the journey of life. Knowledge and experience are the way to wisdom and is a great teacher. When you learn, comprehend the information and see if it resonates with the truth. Apply what you have learned. Always be willing to learn.

Use your time and energy wisely. Remember, money is energy. Stay balanced and healthy.

Obey the laws of Nature, and you can live a life that is fulfilling.

True wealth starts within. Build and discover this wealth. Know and master self, and the world around you is mastered.

To the reader,

I hope that you enjoy reading this book and that you have gained tremendous value. Truth is not always told, and I want to be the one to tell the truth and for you to be the one who operates and seeks truth. As truth is perfect harmony, it can guide us toward better lives, better connections, and overall, a better world. As we live in a mental world, we must be conscious of and protect our energy.

Remember to learn, study, research, see if what you've learned resonates with the truth. If what you've learned resonates with the truth and inspires you to live better, accomplish your goals, etc., then apply what is learned. Be a student and teacher of life.

If you have any questions, testimonials, comments, etc., feel free to email zacharycurtis47@gmail.com. I offer consultation services, mainly to assist with growing spiritually and in life.

Much love, health, wealth, happiness, and prosperity to you. May you continue thriving, be the best you, and let your light shine.

Sincerely,

CPSIA information can be obtained
at www.ICGtesting.com
Printed in the USA
LVHW081523100222
710600LV00011B/412

9 781639 371501